Tough Puzzles
for Smart Kids

By Terry Stickels

imagine!
Publishing

Special thanks to Christy Davis, Elizabeth Anne Baker, Terry Baughan, Anthony Immanuvel, and Sam Bellotto Jr.

10 9 8 7 6 5 4 3

An Imagine Book
Published by Charlesbridge
85 Main Street
Watertown, MA 02472
617-926-0329
www.charlesbridge.com

ISBN 13: 978-1-936140-40-4

1. What runs but cannot walk, has a mouth but cannot eat or talk, has a bed but does not sleep, has depth but cannot think, makes turns but cannot drive, is wet but never gets dry, and has banks but no money?

2. Below is a puzzle called a **TRICKLEDOWN**. The goal of the puzzle is to arrive at the final word by changing one letter per line. Each letter change must result in a new word. Once a letter has been changed, it has to remain that way. There may be more than one answer, but the rules remain the same. See how quickly you can reach the bottom.

Here's an example with its solution:

MALT	MALT
_____	MART
_____	CART
_____	CARD
CORD	CORD

Now you try:

CAST	FACT	CLOCK
_____	_____	_____
_____	_____	_____
_____	_____	_____
BONE	PURE	_____
	SPIRE	

3. The stack of cubes below is the beginning of a 3x3x4 configuration containing a total of 36 cubes. How many more individual cubes are needed to complete the project? All rows and columns run to completion unless you actually see them end.

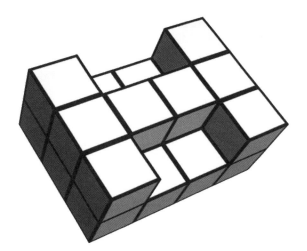

a) 4
b) 12
c) 16
d) 20

4. The numbers in the rectangle below are arranged in such a manner that the last number in each row can be determined from the way the first three numbers of each row are placed. Can you find the pattern and determine the missing numbers?

3	4	12	16
5	1	5	6
7	2	14	16
8	6	?	?

5. Marley the Mouse is about to enter a maze where each block has a rule on how to proceed. The left to right directions are from Marley's point of view, while the north, south, east, and west directions are indicated by the legend below. If the directions tell him to leave a block in a certain direction, he will depart the block in the middle. That is, if he has to turn, he turns in the middle of the block to leave.

What is the letter or number of the block where Marley will exit the maze?

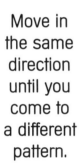

Move in the same direction until you come to a different pattern.

Turn North
90°

Turn Left
90°

Turn Right
90°

Turn East
90°

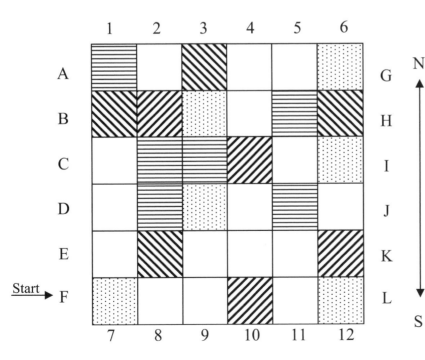

6. The defendant testified, "The attorney is my brother." But the attorney had to take the stand and denied having a brother under oath. Who is lying?

7. What is 1/2 of 1/3 of 1/7 of 42, divided by 1/2, times 2?

8. One of the following figures is different from the rest. Which one and why?

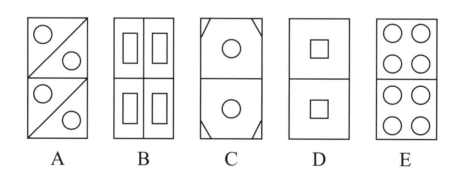

A   B   C   D   E

9. This type of puzzle is called a **WORDOKU**. Fill the grid with letters in such a way that all rows and columns have all letters once and only once. No two letters can be in the same row, column, or 3x3 box. One of the answers is the keyword: a nine-letter word that is correctly spelled out. It can be horizontal or vertical, and the keyword may be spelled backward. Below is an example. The keyword is WORKPLACE.

	L	E		R				P
A		P						
			A	O				
	R		C	E	O	L		
		L				P		
		A	L	P	K		O	
				K	E			
					K		E	
R				C		W	L	

O	L	E	K	R	C	A	W	P
A	K	P	E	W	L	O	C	R
C	W	R	A	O	P	E	K	L
P	R	W	C	E	O	L	A	K
K	O	L	R	A	W	P	E	C
E	C	A	L	P	K	R	O	W
L	P	O	W	K	E	C	R	A
W	A	C	O	L	R	K	P	E
R	E	K	P	C	A	W	L	O

Now you try. The keyword is CHAMPIONS.

					H		P	C
		O		N				H
						O	N	
		C		O	P	N	M	
	O						S	
	M	I	H	S		C		
	P	H						
I				M		P		
M	A		P					

10. This type of puzzle is called a **FRAME GAME**. Can you find the hidden word or phrase in the frame?

11. Your mother's sister's daughter's brother is your:

a)   Uncle
b)   Cousin
c)   Nephew
d)   Niece
e)   Father

12. What letter comes next? Here's a hint: Seven out of twelve.

J   J   A   S   O   N   **?**

13. You are driving a bus. Five people get on and eight people get off. Then two people get on and nine people get off. Then twelve people get on and four more people get off. What color are the bus driver's eyes?

14. In the figure below, which black line is bent more—the one on top or the one on the bottom?

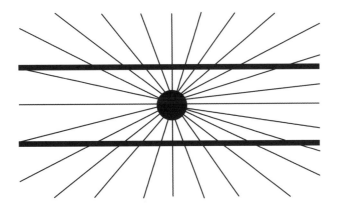

15. All kinds of fun puzzles have been created by inserting plus and minus signs between the digits 1 through 9. For example:

$9 + 8 + 7 + 65 + 4 + 3 + 2 + 1 = 99$

There's at least one other way to create an equation that equals 99. Can you find it?

16. This kind of puzzle is called a **SQUEEZER**. One word will fit between the two given words on each line . . . making two new words: one from the back, one from the front. (The number of spaces represents the number of letters in the **SQUEEZER** word.)

Example: FIRE _ _ _ _WORK

FIRE w o o d WORK

Now you try:

1. TIME ____ ____ ____ ____ ____ CLOTH

2. SHORE ____ ____ ____ ____ BACKER

3. CARD ____ ____ ____ ____ ____ WALK

17. Use the clues below to find the number being described:

I am a four-digit number.
My tens digit is five more than my ones digit but both numbers are squares.
My hundreds digit is six less than my tens digit.
My thousands digit is one half the total of the sum of the other three digits.

What number am I?

18. There are three pairs of identical elephants and an odd one.
Can you find the odd one?

A

B

C

D

E

F

G

19. This kind of puzzle is called a **FUTOSHIKI**. Place digits 1–5 in the grid. Each row and column should have all digits once and only once. The ❯ (greater than) and ❮ (lesser than) symbols between cells indicate which cell has a larger number.

Here's an example with its solution:

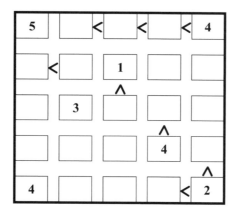
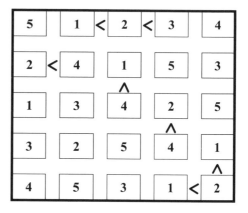

Now you try:

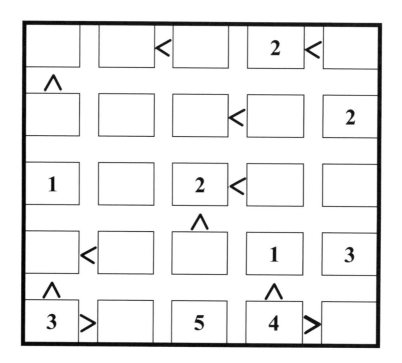

20.

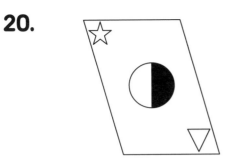

Choose the figure that is the mirror image of the figure above.

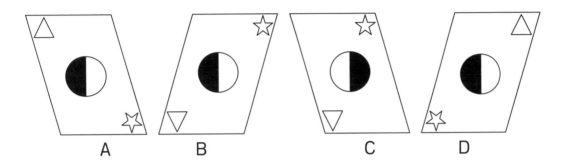

A   B   C   D

21. Using any math symbols or operations you choose, can you complete the following:

1) Use three 1s to form an expression that equals 0.
2) Use three 4s to form an expression that equals 11.
3) Use three 9s to form an expression that equals 15.
4) Use three 5s to form an expression that equals 6.

22. How many times does the letter "F" appear below?

Forever figuring fancy new ways to catch fish by refining their flies, the finest forty Finnish fishermen compete for honors in frigid conditions for four days. Just fractions of a pound separate them.

23. Below are three views of the same cube. Can you figure out what letter is opposite B?

24. What letter is below the letter three letters to the right of the letter above the letter K?

A	B	C	D	E
F	G	H	I	J
K	L	M	N	O
P	Q	R	S	T
U	V	W	X	Y

25. One of the figures below does not belong with the other four figures based on a simple, straightforward design feature. Which figure is the odd one out?

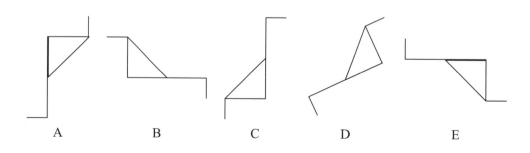

A   B   C   D   E

26. An anagram is a word whose letters can be rearranged to form a new word. One example is the word "sneak." Its letters can be made to spell "snake." Another example is "poodle." Its letters can be made to spell "pooled" or "looped."

Here is a list of words whose anagrams spell the names of animals. See how many you can come up with:

a) sale
b) shore
c) flow
d) trees
e) paroled
f) greet

27. A horse travels the same distance every day. Oddly, two of its legs travel farther than the other two legs every day. This is not a trick, nor is it a play on words. This has actually happened. Since the horse is normal, how is this situation possible?

28. Each block below is the same size, and each block has six faces. How many other blocks does the face or side of each block touch? Blocks that connect at the edges or corners don't count.

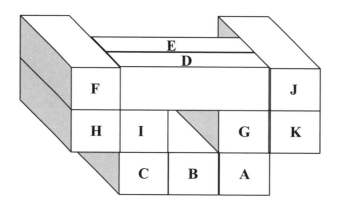

29. The number in the middle of each grid is a result of operations performed on the other four numbers. The operations are the same for each box. What number goes in the last box?

10		12
	15	
19		4

13		6
	18	
27		8

30		2
	20	
11		17

25		35
	24	
9		3

6		4
	?	
21		5

30. Below are three more **SQUEEZER** puzzles. Can you find the missing word for each?

a) TEAM ____ ____ ____ ____ SHOP

b) SLING ____ ____ ____ ____ GUN

c) SPOT ____ ____ ____ ____ ____ WEIGHT

31. Jamie's mom bought him a bottle of juice that weighs 36 ounces. "I wonder how much is juice and how much is the weight of the bottle by itself," Jamie said. "Funny you should bring that up, because I wondered the same thing when I was buying it," his mom replied. "So I asked the store manager and he said the weight of the juice is half as much as the weight of the bottle."

If that is true, how much does the juice weigh?

32. Find the hidden word or phrase in this *FRAME GAME*:

33. Here's a puzzle that appears more difficult than it is . . . if you just take the time to think about it a different way. Solving this one takes that special AHA! moment of insight.

If Linda walks to work and rides back home, it takes her 3 hours total. When she rides both ways, it takes her 1 hour and 15 minutes. How long would it take her to make the round trip by walking?

34. You may know the old saying, "Two wrongs don't make a right." But in this alphametic puzzle where letters equal numbers, three wrongs add up to a right. Your job is to find the values of the numbers. We'll give you some hints by providing the number values of several letters.

G = 2 and O = 0. There is no 5 or 7. No word can begin with zero. Each letter has a unique value.

$$
\begin{array}{r}
WRONG \\
WRONG \\
+\ WRONG \\
\hline
RIGHT
\end{array}
$$

35. Here is another **WORDOKU**. The keyword is MACHINERY.

	E	R			Y			N
				C				
	I	A					R	
					N			
	N	C	Y	A	M	I	E	
			E					
	A						E	M
				Y				
R			C				Y	I

36. How many individual boards are in the configuration below? There are no hidden boards, and all boards are the same length.

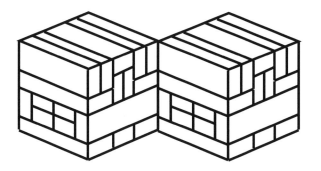

37. Here are three more **TRICKLEDOWN** puzzles. Can you find the solutions?

REST   MAJOR   GROWN

_____   _____   _____

_____   _____   _____

_____   _____   _____

PAWS   _____   _____

                DINES   CHESS

38. Martha, Mike, and Moosaca are going to play a series of one-set tennis single matches against each other. The winner of each set stays on the court and plays the player who had been idle. The loser of each set sits out the next match. At the end of the week, Martha played 15 sets, Mike played 14 sets, and Moosaca played 9 sets. Who played the eleventh set?

39. Can you fill in the missing letters to complete the names of the countries?

Here's an example: G R _ _ C _
                    Answer: G R E E C E

a) B E ____ ____ ____ U ____

b) N ____ C ____ R A ____ ____ ____

c) ____ O M A N ____ ____

d) G ____ R ____ ____ N Y

e) A U ____ T ____ ____ L ____ ____

40. Below is a grid with four symbols. Each symbol has a different number value. No number is greater than five, and each line adds up to the number at its end. Can you find the value for each symbol? The number twelve in the corner is the sum of the diagonal.

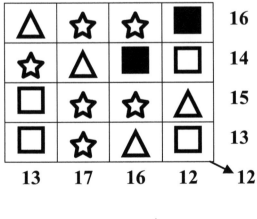

Here's a hint: The △ is 2.

41. What one word can be placed before the three words below to make three new words?

1) SLED
2) WHITE
3) CAT

42. Below is a triangle where each side has a sum of 17. This triangle uses the numbers 1–10, and the number in the middle is not counted in any side's sum.

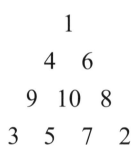

```
            1
         4    6
      9   10   8
    3   5   7   2
```

It turns out that 17 is the smallest sum possible of any side. What is the largest sum any side can have using the numbers 1–10? Can you create the triangle? Here's a hint to get you started. The largest sum of a side is more than 25.

43. The five items below all share a common characteristic. Can you name it?

skillet   pail   hairbrush   briefcase   lantern

44. Young Stars

Across

1 Droop in the middle
4 Comic actor Allen who starred in *The Santa Clause*
7 Word on a school bus
11 Spanish hooray
12 Catholic leader who lives in the Vatican
13 Simba's hair
14 Ginger _____
15 TV's _____ *Square Pants*
17 Black-and-white bear from China
19 Not sharp
20 Slow-moving garden creatures in shells
22 Pop singer Gomez who performs with The Scene
26 Proud
28 Homework assignment
29 _____-hop music
32 Item in a broom closet
34 Seashell seller in a tongue twister
35 Get a new pet from the animal shelter
38 Gift-wrapping need
41 _____ picture
43 Demi who stars on TV's *Sonny With a Chance*
47 Chew like a beaver
49 Identified a new pet
50 Miranda Cosgrove's character on Nickelodeon
54 ". . . _____ a partridge in a pear tree"
55 Garfield's playmate in comics
56 Dog in *The Wizard of Oz*
57 Muppet girl monster in a tutu
58 Burst into tears
59 Turkey Day veggie
60 Mistake

Down

1 Daytime TV serials
2 Edgar _____ Poe
3 Actress Davis in *Stuart Little*
4 Spinning toy
5 Popular MP3 music player from Apple
6 Computer program features
7 Stinks
8 Chemistry classroom
9 Sean Lennon's middle name
10 Kind of page on the Internet
12 Sacred song sung in church
16 High school club
18 Trash-talk
21 Grade-school calculation
23 Superman's logo
24 "Uh-uh!"
25 Jack Sparrow's "yes"
27 *You've _____ Mail*
29 *Green Eggs and _____* by Dr. Seuss
30 *Who Wants to Be a Millionaire* response
31 Tea container
33 Schoolmate
36 Friend of Pooh and Roo
37 Broadway award for *The Lion King*
39 Cartoon movie about a goldfish who turns into a little girl
40 Spacewalk, to NASA
42 Bad, as weather
44 Knock one's socks off
45 Voice above baritone
46 More unusual
48 Command to stop a horse
50 Milk source on the farm
51 Fruity summer beverage
52 Tear apart
53 Money machine outside the bank

45. How observant are you? Below are things we see all the time. But do we really pay attention when we look at these things?

a) The one dollar bill has the word ONE written on the back of it—centered in the middle. The five dollar bill has Abraham Lincoln on the front and _____ on the back—centered in the middle.

b) On a standard keyboard, what letter is between "V" and "N"?

c) The inauguration of an American president is always on _____ unless that day falls on a Sunday.

d) Name the seventh dwarf: Bashful, Sleepy, Happy, Grumpy, Dopey, Doc, and . . .

46. On the dice below, the opposite faces total seven. But one of the pictures is incorrect because of the *orientation* of the dots. Which die is incorrect, and why?

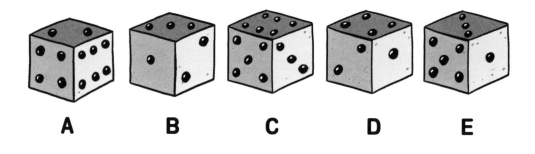

| A | B | C | D | E |

47. This kind of puzzle is called a **LETTER LINK**. Your job is to connect adjacent letters within the triangle to form words of at least three letters. Each letter may be used once and only once for each word. Any letter that has one of its three sides touching another letter is considered to be an adjacent letter. Likewise, the point of any triangle touching another triangle point is considered to be adjacent.

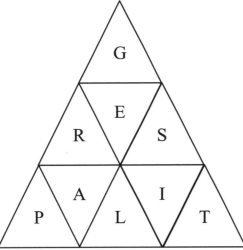

Examples:
  1) The letters R, E, S, I, L, and A are all touching each other.
  2) The letter G touches R, E, and S.
  3) The letter T touches L, I, and S.

Your goal is to come up with as many words as you can. Remember, they must be at least three letters long.

48. Using two regular six-sided cubes to show the days of the month, how can the numbers be arranged on each cube to show every possible day? Each day must show two numbers. For example, the seventh day of any month must be 07.

49. Find the hidden word or phrase in the **FRAME GAME** below:

50. The five items below all share a common characteristic. Can you name it?

grandfather clock

golf club

Mona Lisa

playing cards

moon (humorously)

51. Your mom loves to go to antique shops and buy and sell antique lamps. She has asked you to come along to be her "calculator" and to let her know where she stands with her lamp deals.

She started the day by buying two antique lamps for $60 each. Later, she was offered $70 for one of the lamps and she sold it. Later that afternoon, she saw that a similar lamp to the one she sold was being sold for $90, so she bought back the lamp she had sold in the morning for $80. She then sold it for $90. The second lamp she had purchased in the morning didn't sell so your mom reduced the price by 10 percent of her purchase price and it finally sold at the reduced price. Your mom then purchased a lamp for $100 and sold it for $160. At this point in the day, is your mom ahead, behind, or even with her purchases and sales?

52. Can you arrange the numbers in the boxes so that no two consecutive numbers are next to each other (horizontally, vertically, or diagonally)?

1	2	
3	4	5
6	7	8
	9	10

53. A basketball team uses a rotation of eight players, with only five being on the court at any one time. All games consist of twelve-minute quarters. Below is a list of players and the minutes each played in the last game, with the exception of one player's time. How many minutes did Pellini play?

	Name	Minutes
1)	Anson	34
2)	O'Malley	29
3)	Garren	30
4)	Fortis	36
5)	Aziz	27
6)	Rodriguez	31
7)	Stinson	35
8)	Pellini	?

54. Remove only three toothpicks and leave three triangles.

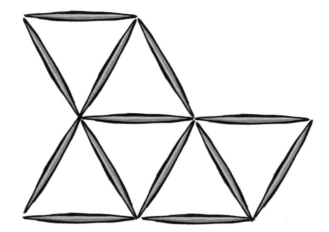

55. Which line is an extension of the line starting in the upper left hand portion of the picture below?

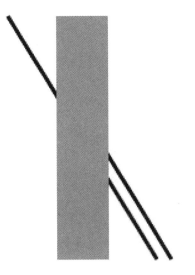

56. I have a seven-gallon bucket and a five-gallon bucket. Using these two buckets only, I need exactly six gallons of water. Can this be accomplished?

57. In the number square below, the same rule applies in two ways— from top to bottom and from left to right. What is the missing number?

3	8	11
4	5	9
7	13	?

58. This kind of puzzle is called **UP & DOWN WORDS**. Look at the clue to solve number 1. The second part of the answer to number 1 is the first part of the answer to number 2. That continues all the way to the end. Here's an example:

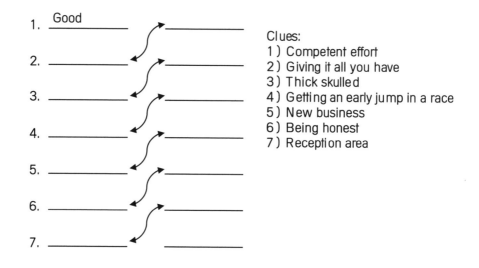

Clues:
1) Competent effort
2) Giving it all you have
3) Thick skulled
4) Getting an early jump in a race
5) New business
6) Being honest
7) Reception area

Here's the answer:

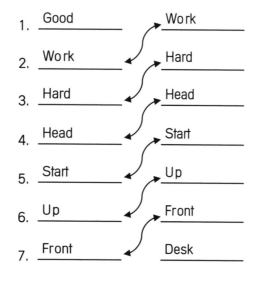

Now, try this:

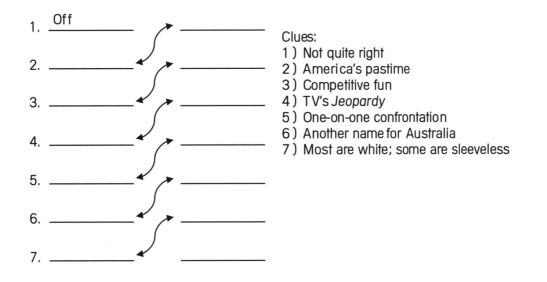

1. Off _____ _____
2. _____ _____
3. _____ _____
4. _____ _____
5. _____ _____
6. _____ _____
7. _____ _____

Clues:
1) Not quite right
2) America's pastime
3) Competitive fun
4) TV's *Jeopardy*
5) One-on-one confrontation
6) Another name for Australia
7) Most are white; some are sleeveless

59. This kind of puzzle is called *MISSING PAIRS*. Each puzzle has two sets of blanks. Your job is to fill in those blanks with the same pair of letters to complete a common, well-known word. Here are two examples:

1) C _ _ k b _ _ k   Answer: Cookbook
2) _ _ p _ _ zard   Answer: Haphazard

Try these:

1) M ____ ____ h ____ ____ dle

2) ____ ____ d e r g r o ____ ____ d

3) S ____ ____ v ____ ____ s

4) A ____ ____ d v ____ ____ k

60. A gecko is trying to crawl up a drain spout but keeps sliding back. After each minute, he moves three feet up the spout only to fall back two feet. The spout is twenty feet high. How long will it take the gecko to reach the top?

61. Below are three more **SQUEEZER** puzzles. Can you find the missing word for each?

1. POST ____ ____ ____ ____ BOARD

2. HOUSE ____ ____ ____ ____ HOUSE

3. GRAND ____ ____ ____ ____ ____ PROOF

62. Here's another alphametic puzzle. E = 4, P = 6, and X = 0. There is no 9. Remember, no word can begin with zero.

$$\begin{array}{r} ALEX \\ PLAY \\ PLAY \\ + PLAY \\ \hline BEATS \end{array}$$

63. If the stack of cubes below was originally 3x3x3, which of the pieces below is the missing piece of the cube? Note: All rows and columns run to completion unless you actually see them end. The missing piece is to be inserted upside down to complete the cube.

A

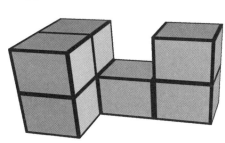

B

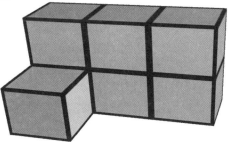

C

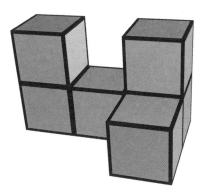

D

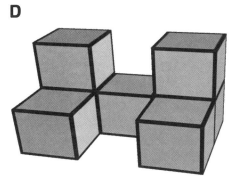

64. This kind of puzzle is called **SPLIT WORDS**. There are four words of six letters each scrambled in the pairings of letters below. The letters found in each group appear together in the original word. For example, the word monkey would be broken into *mo*, *nk*, and *ey*. It's your job to find those scrambled letters and put them together to make the word monkey. For this first set, one of the four words is *minute*.

LS	LF	WE
TO	BU	ER
MI	**TE**	LE
CK	GO	**NU**

65. The scrambled letters in each section of the square use the center letter to make a different nine-letter word. Can you unscramble the letters and fgure out what each word is?

66. Jake is at the local mall and has a chance to win a new cell phone if he can answer the following question. He can pick one person to help him and he has chosen you! Can you help Jake win the phone? Here's the puzzle:

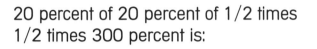

20 percent of 20 percent of 1/2 times 1/2 times 300 percent is:

a) .4
b) 1
c) .03
d) 13

67. Can you connect the dots below together in a continuous line? Only vertical or horizontal lines can be used and all lines must connect two dots together. No lines can cross each other. The starting line has been drawn for you.

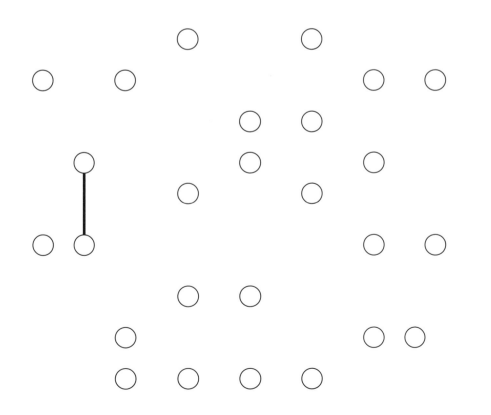

68. Here is another Marley the Mouse puzzle.

Marley enters the maze and moves from left to right. The left to right directions are from his point of view, while the north, south, east, and west directions are indicated by the legend below. If the directions tell him to leave a block in a certain direction, he will depart the block in the middle. That is, if he has to turn, he turns in the middle of the block to leave.

What is the letter or number of the block where Marley will exit?

| Turn East 90° | Move in the same direction until you come to a different pattern. | Turn North 90° | Turn Left 90° | Turn South 90° | Turn Right 90° |

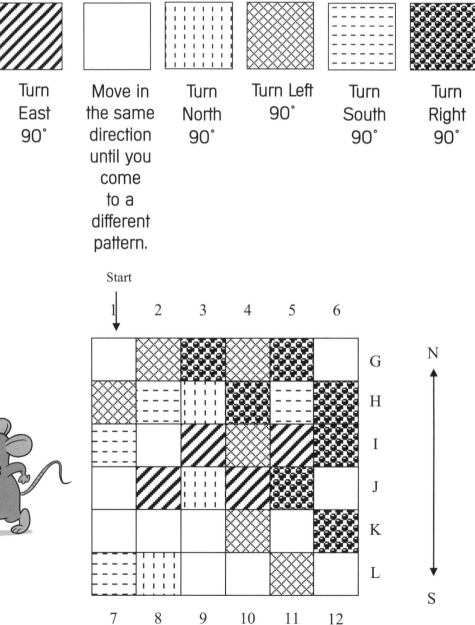

36

69. Monkeys and leopards are natural enemies in the jungle. Monkeys are safest in the trees and warn each other when the leopards hunt in their territory. But any monkey caught on the ground is in danger when leopards are hunting. Draw six straight lines across the square below to separate the leopards from the monkeys. When the lines have been drawn, no section containing a leopard can also have monkeys in it. The lines cannot cut off any part of the monkeys or leopards.

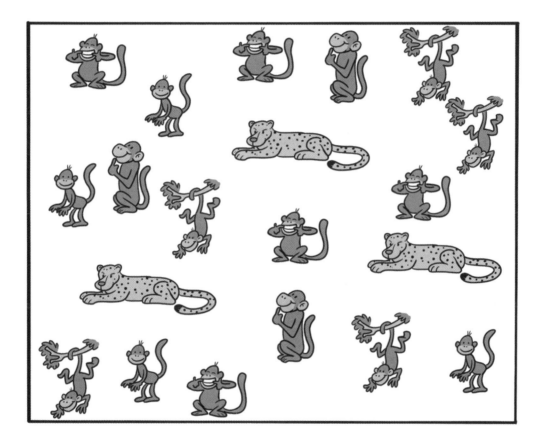

70. The phrase "STAY IN SACK" is an anagram of an American:

    a) City
    b) Professional golfer
    c) Musician
    d) State

71. Read the sign below quickly, then say it out loud. What does it say?

72. Below are six nine-letter words with the vowels in place but no consonants. The scrambled consonants for each word are listed to the left of the word. Can you put the consonants in the right places to reveal each of the nine-letter words?

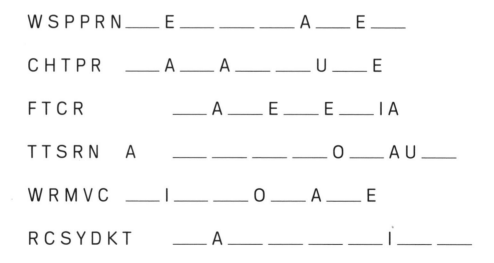

W S P P R N ___ E ___ ___ ___ A ___ E ___

C H T P R ___ A ___ A ___ ___ U ___ E

F T C R ___ A ___ E ___ E ___ I A

T T S R N A ___ ___ ___ ___ O ___ A U ___

W R M V C ___ I ___ ___ O ___ A ___ E

R C S Y D K T ___ A ___ ___ ___ ___ I ___ ___

73. Christy owns a pet shop where she sells cats. If she puts one cat in each cage, she has one cat too many. If she puts two cats in each cage, she has one cage too many. How many cats and cages does Christy have?

74. If you were to cut the square below into two pieces, would it be possible to move the star into the center of the square when you rearranged the pieces?

75. This puzzle has been turned into a jigsaw puzzle! The completed grid has been broken into smaller number-pieces and placed around the page. Put the number-pieces back into the grid so that every row (across) equals twelve and every column (down) equals ten.

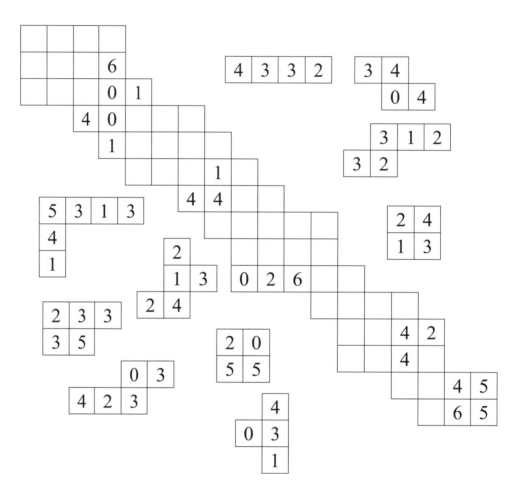

76. There are fifteen words hidden in the grid below. The words can go horizontally, vertically, or diagonally, and may run forward or backward. Can you find them all?

PREPOSITIONS

```
G  L  L  T  Q  Y  T  D  N  O  Y  E  B
N  T  D  D  G  R  M  G  T  T  G  Q  H
T  O  R  T  A  M  O  N  G  N  N  K  L
H  W  A  M  P  O  P  P  O  S  I  T  E
R  A  O  O  Z  E  N  Q  K  M  W  H  N
O  R  B  L  U  G  C  B  R  B  O  N  H
U  D  A  E  M  T  E  X  L  E  L  V  M
G  M  K  O  N  T  S  B  E  S  L  D  K
H  Q  R  T  W  E  B  I  K  I  O  J  E
G  F  N  E  A  R  A  L  D  D  F  V  F
N  W  E  W  F  C  H  T  W  E  O  L  R
X  N  R  N  M  K  G  R  H  B  X  J  M
G  Q  W  W  L  B  B  R  A  M  D  Q  L
```

Aboard	Between	Near
Above	Beyond	Opposite
Among	Except	Outside
Beneath	Following	Through
Beside	From	Toward

77. Can you arrange the numbers 1–7 in such a way that they are in three straight lines, and each line adds up to twelve?

78. What one word can be placed before the four words below to make four new words?

1) PLACE
2) WOOD
3) FLY
4) PROOF

79. Below is a grid with four symbols. Each symbol has a different number value. No number is greater than eight, and each line adds up to the number at its end. Can you find the value for each symbol? The number in the corner is the sum of the diagonal.

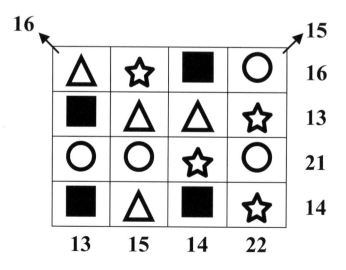

80. In a kingdom far, far away, there is a prince who always tells the truth, a princess who sometimes tells the truth, and a court jester who never tells the truth. Below are three statements, one by each of them. The characters are standing in the order of the statements.

    1) "The prince is next to me."
    2) "I am the princess."
    3) "The court jester is next to me."

Who made each statement?

81. This kind of puzzle is called **WORD SPLIT**. Below are eight four-letter words. Each word is split in half to make two-letter pairs. For example, DOOR would be shown as DO and OR. These two-letter pairs can be found in the box below, in no particular order. Put the pairs together to find the eight four-letter words. None of the letters may be used more than once unless they appear in the box more than once.

PA	RK	LP	AR
OM	BE	ZO	JE
RA	SP	GU	WE
ST	VE	IT	ER

_____ _____ _____
_____ _____
_____ _____
_____ _____

82. Below are three squares of the same size and dimension. Can you put them together to create seven squares? The seven squares do not have to be the same size.

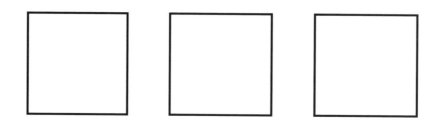

83. Here are three more **TRICKLEDOWN** puzzles. Can you find the solutions?

CHIP	CHUNK	CLASS
_____	_____	_____
_____	_____	_____
_____	_____	_____
SLAM	_____	_____
	SLICE	GROWN

84. Can you place the numbers 1–16 in a grid so that no two consecutive numbers are next to each other horizontally, vertically, or diagonally? We've given you five numbers to start. There may be more than one way to accomplish this.

12			2
		14	
4			11

85. There are four pairs of zebras in this picture. Can you find the odd one out?

A

B

C

D

E

F

G

H

I

86. The figures below all follow the same pattern. Using that pattern, can you find the missing number?

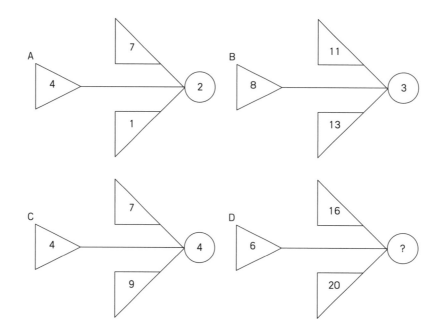

87. Can you place the numbers 1–10 in the figure below so the two rows and two columns have the same sum? The numbers 8 and 1 have been placed for you to give you a head start.

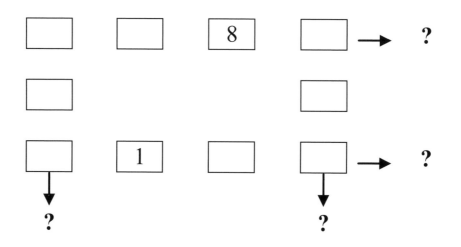

88. How many triangles of any size are in the configuration below?

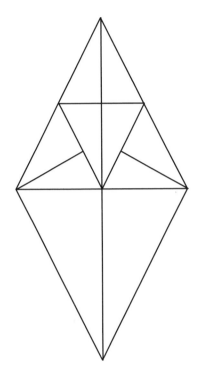

89. Here's another **SPLIT WORDS** puzzle. One of the words is **pretty**.

RD	EN	SI
ON	RD	**TY**
GA	ER	BO
VI	**ET**	**PR**

90. Can you arrange the five pieces below to form a square?

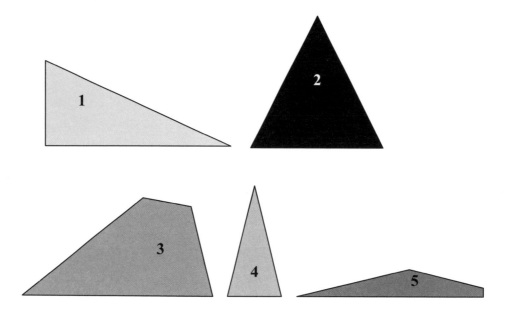

91. Here is another **FUTOSHIKI**. Place digits 1–5 in the grid. Each row and column should have all digits once and only once. The ⟩ (greater than) and ⟨ (lesser than) symbols between cells indicate which cell has a larger number.

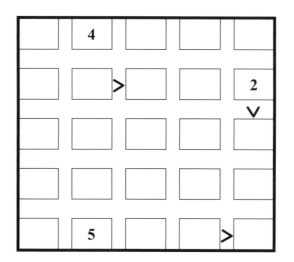

92. Below are twenty-four toothpicks arranged in a 3x3 grid. What is the minimum number of toothpicks that need to be removed so there are no squares of any size remaining in the grid? There may be more than one way to solve this, but the minimum number of toothpicks that need to be removed is always the same.

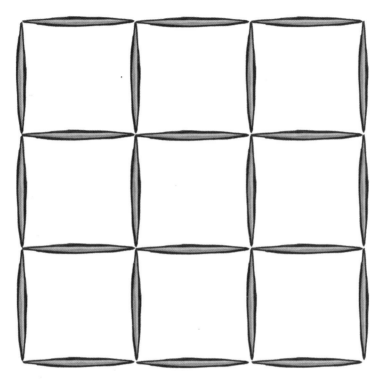

93. Based on the first three triangles, what number should replace the question mark?

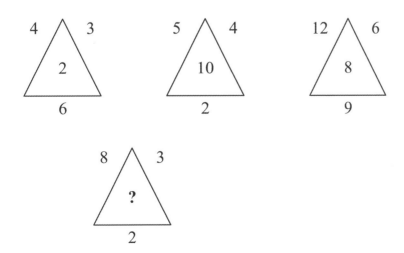

94. Here is another Marley the Mouse puzzle.

Marley enters the maze and moves from left to right. The left to right directions are from his point of view, while the north, south, east, and west directions are indicated by the map legend. If the directions tell him to leave a block in a certain direction, he will depart the block in the middle. That is, if he has to turn, he turns in the middle of the block to leave.

What is the letter or number of the block where Marley will exit?

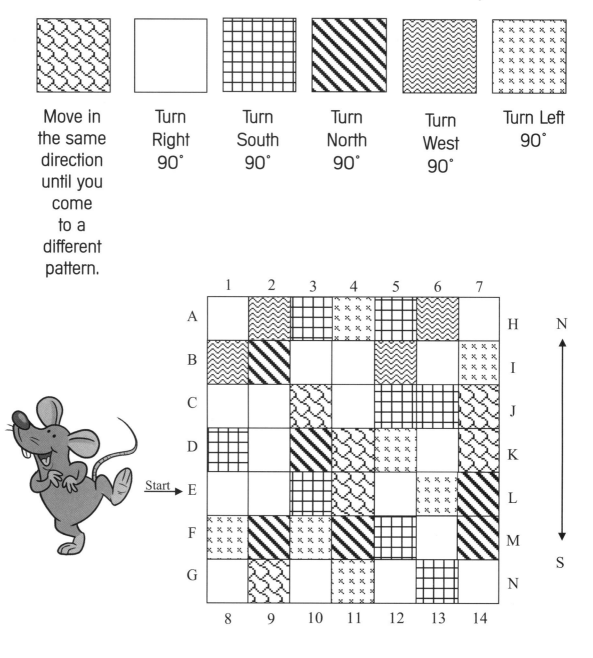

95. What will happen to each weight (A and B) when the rightmost gear turns in the direction of the arrow?

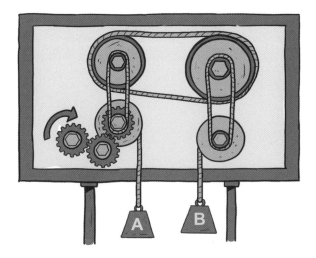

96. Find the hidden word or phrase in this *FRAME GAME*:

97.

At The Zoo

```
Y   N   C   L   X   P   R   M   Y   D   V   S
E   O   F   H   B   F   L   G   R   P   R   U
K   I   L   J   E   R   R   A   Z   P   S   M
N   L   M   N   N   E   P   L   O   D   O   A
O   C   T   A   C   O   T   L   Z   P   R   T
M   N   W   H   E   R   A   A   V   A   E   O
P   S   R   L   M   R   U   N   H   N   C   P
H   D   K   P   B   C   X   M   P   D   O   O
P   G   N   E   M   Y   D   V   E   A   N   P
F   F   A   L   F   C   L   B   M   L   I   P
P   R   K   J   T   M   W   O   L   F   H   I
B   R   A   E   B   A   L   A   O   K   R   H
```

Cheetah	Leopard	Polar Bear
Hippopotamus	Lion	Rhinoceros
Koala Bear	Monkey	Swan
Lemur	Panda	Wolf

98. Magic squares are some of the best puzzles to solve. The sum of each row, column, and diagonal must total the same. Here is the beginning of a 5x5 magic square. See if you can fill in the missing numbers. The numbers 1 through 25 are used for this particular puzzle. Each number may only be used once. Every row, column, and diagonal should total 65.

9			5	17
3	20			
	14	1	18	10
		25	12	4
15	2			23

99. Here are three more **TRICKLEDOWN** puzzles. Can you find the solutions?

SORT   BLINK   HANDS

_____   _____   _____

_____   _____   _____

_____   _____   _____

PASS   _____   _____

               TRACE   BEARD

100. One of the words below does not belong with the other words based on any one of three different reasons. See if you can find the odd word out based on at least one of the reasons.

Rainwater   Numerical   Acceptable
Backboard   Showering   Textbooks

Answers

1. A river.

2. Remember, there may be more than one answer:

CAST	FACT	CLOCK
CASE	PACT	CLICK
BASE	PACE	SLICK
BANE	PARE	SLICE
BONE	PURE	SPICE
	SPIRE	

3. c) 16

4. 48 and 54
The rule is to multiply the first two numbers in each row to get the third number. Then add the second number and the third number in each row together to get the last number.

5. Marley will exit at block 1.

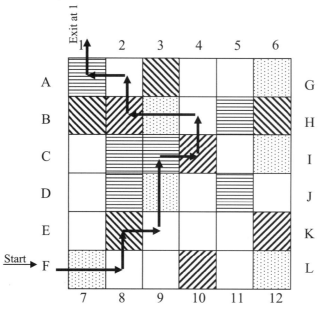

6. No one is lying. The defendant was his sister.

7. 4

1/7 of 42 = 6
1/3 of 6 = 2
1/2 of 2 = 1
1 divided by 1/2 = 2
and 2x2 = 4

8. A

Figures B, C, D, and E are mirror images. (The top and bottom halves are reflections of each other.)

9.

S	N	M	O	A	H	I	P	C
P	I	O	C	N	S	M	A	H
C	H	A	M	P	I	O	N	S
H	S	C	I	O	P	N	M	A
A	O	P	N	C	M	H	S	I
N	M	I	H	S	A	C	O	P
O	P	H	S	I	N	A	C	M
I	C	S	A	M	O	P	H	N
M	A	N	P	H	C	S	I	O

10. Balanced Meals

11. b) Cousin
Your mother has a sister, who is your aunt. Your aunt has a daughter, who is your cousin. That cousin has a brother, who is also your cousin.

12. D
These are the first letters of the names of the months in consecutive order beginning with June.

13. Whatever color your eyes are. You are driving the bus, remember?

14. Neither is bent. Both are straight and parallel to each other!

15. 9 + 8 + 7 + 6 + 5 + 43 + 21 = 99

16. 1. Table
2. Line
3. Board

17. 8,394

18. F
The pairs are A-E (tips of tails are missing and the areas to the right of the trunks are colored in); B-C (the right ears are different from the rest); D-G (the middle toes on hind foot are colored in).

19.

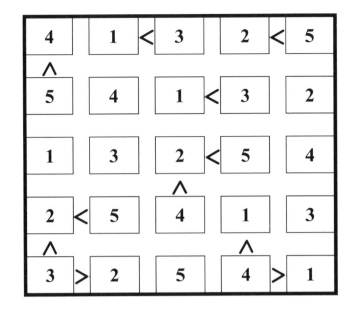

20. B

21. 1) 1/1 - 1 = 0 or 1 - 1/1 = 0 or (1 x 1) - 1 = 0

2) 44/4 = 11

3) $9 + \sqrt{9} + \sqrt{9} = 9 + 3 + 3 = 15$

4) 5/5 + 5 = 6

22. Sixteen times
① ② ③ ④ ⑤
Forever figuring fancy new ways to catch fish by refining their
⑥ ⑦ ⑧ ⑨ ⑩ ⑪
flies, the finest forty Finnish fishermen compete for honors
⑫ ⑬ ⑭ ⑮ ⑯
in frigid conditions for four days. Just fractions of a pound

separate them.

23. Y

Look at figures 2 and 3. Y is surrounded by F and Z on figure 2 and I and O on figure 3. Since there are six total faces on the cube, that leaves face B as the only option to be opposite face Y.

24. N

Working backward, the letter above K is F. Three letters to the right of F is I. And the letter below I is N.

25. D

When rotated properly, the other figures all have a "P" figure that looks like this: $\vdash$. D has a "P" that looks like this: $\urcorner$

26. a) sale = seal
b) shore = horse
c) flow = wolf
d) trees = steer
e) paroled = leopard
f) greet = egret

27. The horse operates a mill and travels in a circular manner all day long. The two outside legs will travel a greater distance than the two inside legs.

28. A = 2; B = 2; C = 2; D = 5; E = 5; F = 3; G = 4; H = 2; I = 4; J = 3; K = 2.

29. 12

Add the four corner numbers in each box and divide the sum by three to get the number in the middle.

30. a) Work
b) Shot
c) Light

31. The bottle (with the juice) weighs 36 ounces, so the bottle by itself weighs 24 ounces and the juice weighs 12 ounces.

32. One Step Forward, Two Steps Backward

33. It would take her 4 hours and 45 minutes. If Linda made two round trips the first way, it would take her 6 hours. That is, she would cover the distance twice by walking and twice by riding. So 6 hours minus 1 hour and 15 minutes, or 4 hours and 45 minutes, will be the total time walking both ways.

34. G = 2; H = 4; I = 9; N = 8; O = 0; R = 3; T = 6; W = 1

$$
\begin{array}{r}
13082 \\
13082 \\
+\,13082 \\
\hline
39246
\end{array}
$$

35.

C	E	R	A	I	Y	M	H	N
N	H	M	R	C	E	A	Y	I
Y	I	A	N	M	H	C	R	E
A	Y	E	I	R	N	H	C	M
H	N	C	Y	A	M	I	E	R
M	R	I	E	H	C	N	A	Y
I	A	Y	H	N	R	E	M	C
E	C	H	M	Y	I	R	N	A
R	M	N	C	E	A	Y	I	H

36. 36

37. Remember, there may be more than one answer:

REST	MAJOR	GROWN
PEST	MANOR	CROWN
PAST	MINOR	CROWS
PASS	MINER	CREWS
PAWS	DINER	CHEWS
	DINES	CHESS

38. Martha and Mike played the eleventh set.

The total number of sets played was $\frac{(15+14+9)}{2} = \frac{38}{2} = 19$ sets. Moosaca played 9 sets and sat out 10 sets, which means he lost the even numbered sets, leaving Martha and Mike as the players of the eleventh set.

39. a) Belgium
b) Nicaragua
c) Romania
d) Germany
e) Australia

40. $\triangle = 2$, $\square = 3$, $\blacksquare = 4$, $\star = 5$

Look at the second column, which equals 17. We know that $\triangle$ = 2. That means the other three symbols must add up to 15. Since all three symbols are the same, divide the 15 by three to find that $\star$ = 5. Now look at the first row, which equals 16. Two $\star$ plus one $\triangle$ = 12. That means $\blacksquare$ = 4. Finally, look at the third row, which equals 15. We know that two $\star$ plus one $\triangle$ = 2. That means $\square$ = 3.

41. Bob
BOBSLED
BOBWHITE
BOBCAT

42. The largest sum of any side is 27. Here's one triangle showing this but there are many ways this can be accomplished.

43. All have handles.

44.

S	A	G			T	I	M		S	L	O	W
O	L	E		P	O	P	E		M	A	N	E
A	L	E		S	P	O	N	G	E	B	O	B
P	A	N	D	A		D	U	L	L			
S	N	A	I	L	S		S	E	L	E	N	A
		S	M	U	G		E	S	S	A	Y	
H	I	P		M	O	P			S	H	E	
A	D	O	P	T		T	A	P	E			
M	O	T	I	O	N		L	O	V	A	T	O
		G	N	A	W		N	A	M	E	D	
C	A	R	L	Y	S	H	A	Y		A	N	D
O	D	I	E		T	O	T	O		Z	O	E
W	E	P	T		Y	A	M			E	R	R

45. a) The Lincoln Memorial
b) The letter B
c) January 20
d) Sneezy

46. C
The three dots on the side should go across the other diagonal.

47. Here are fifty-seven answers we found. Did you find more?

1. Ail	11. Gear	21. Legs	31. Par	41. Rise	51. Slit
2. Air	12. Gel	22. Lie	32. Pare	42. Sail	52. Tie
3. Aisle	13. Grail	23. Lies	33. Pares	43. Sale	53. Tier
4. Ale	14. Ire	24. Lit	34. Priest	44. Salt	54. Tiers
5. Ales	15. Isle	25. Lost	35. Rail	45. Seal	55. Ties
6. Are	16. Lair	26. Pail	36. Rails	46. Serial	56. Tire
7. Ear	17. Lap	27. Pails	37. Rap	47. Silt	57. Tires
8. Ears	18. Large	28. Pair	38. Real	48. Sir	
9. Era	19. Last	29. Pal	39. Rile	49. Sire	
10. Eras	20. Leg	30. Pale	40. Riles	50. Sit	

48. Each cube has to have 0, 1, and 2 . . . from there it makes no difference where numbers 3, 4, 5, 6, 7, and 8 are placed. They can be placed randomly on the cubes. For number 9, just turn the number 6 upside down.

49. Musically Inclined

50. All have a face.

51. Your mom is currently $74 in the black (ahead). She has spent $300 but taken in $374. Here is a list of her transactions. Each purchase has a minus sign in front; each sale has a plus sign.

-120
+70
-80
+90
+54   This is the second lamp, which she sold for 10 percent off.
-100
+160

One way to total these is to separate the pluses from the minuses:

	+70	
-120	+90	
-80	+54	374
-100	+160	-300
-300	+374	+74

52. Here are two answers. Did you find another way?

10	2	
6	8	5
4	1	3
	7	9

4	2	
6	8	5
10	1	3
	7	9

53. Pellini played 18 minutes. If the same five players were to play a game, there would be a total of 48 x 5 or 240 game-minutes. So, regardless of how many players there are in the course of a game, there must always be 240 game-minutes. The total minutes of the seven players listed before Pellini are 222 minutes, which means Pellini played 18 minutes (222 + 18 = 240).

54.

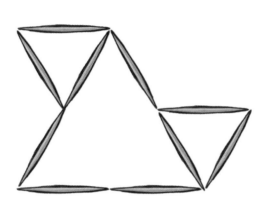

55. The bottom left line.

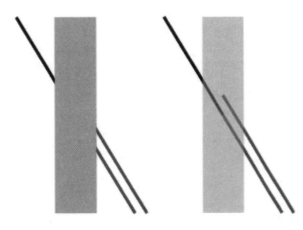

56. Yes, it can. Here's one way:

1. Fill up the five-gallon bucket and pour it into the seven gallon bucket.

2. Fill up the five-gallon bucket again and fill the seven-gallon bucket full, leaving three gallons in the five-gallon bucket.

3. Empty the seven-gallon bucket and pour the three gallons into it.

4. Fill the five-gallon bucket and pour four gallons into the seven-gallon bucket, filling it and leaving one gallon in the five-gallon bucket.

5. Empty the seven-gallon bucket and pour the one gallon left in the five-gallon bucket into the seven-gallon bucket.

6. Now, fill the five-gallon bucket and pour it into the seven gallon bucket, which already has one gallon. That makes six gallons.

57. 20
In each row, from left to right, the first number plus the middle number equals the third number. In each column, beginning at the top and moving toward the bottom, add the top number and the middle number to get the bottom number.

58.

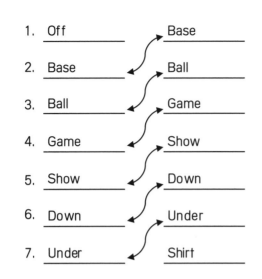

1.	Off	Base
2.	Base	Ball
3.	Ball	Game
4.	Game	Show
5.	Show	Down
6.	Down	Under
7.	Under	Shirt

59.
1) Manhandle
2) Underground
3) Servers
4) Aardvark

60. Eighteen minutes

The gecko proceeds one foot each minute, so after seventeen minutes, it has traveled seventeen feet. In the eighteenth minute, it will climb three feet and reach the top before it slides back two feet.

61. 1. Card
2. Boat
3. Child

62. A = 3; B = 2; E = 4; L = 8; P = 6; S = 1; T = 5; X = 0; Y = 7

```
   3840
   6837
   6837
 + 6837
 ──────
  24351
```

63. Figure C

64. Buckle, Towels, Golfer, Minute

65. Brilliant, Furniture, Hilarious, Curiosity.

66. c) .03
20 percent of 20 percent of 1/2 × 1/2 is the same as .2 × .2 × .5 × .5 or .04 × .25, which equals .01. Multiplying by 300 percent is the same as multiplying by 3. So, .01 × 3 = .03. Did you help Jake win the phone?

67. Here is one solution. Did you find another? As long as the lines don't cross and the connecting lines are either vertical or horizontal, then the solution is valid.

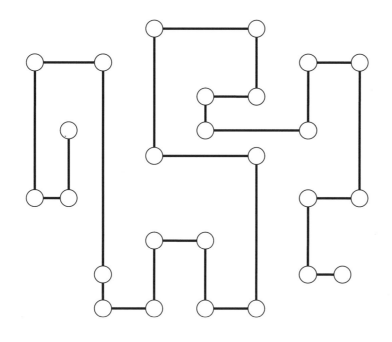

68. Marley will exit at block 10.

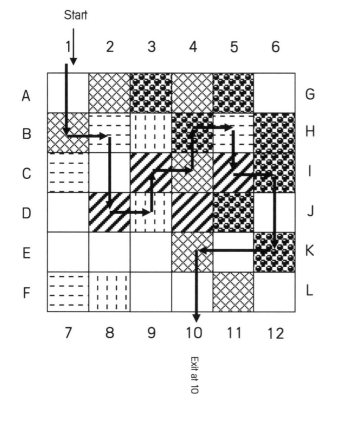

69.

70. a) City

The city is Kansas City.

71. Did you read, "A Bird in the Bush"? Read it again! It says "A Bird in **the the** Bush."

72. NEWSPAPER
PARACHUTE
CAFETERIA
ASTRONAUT
MICROWAVE
YARDSTICK

73. Christy has 4 cats and 3 cages.

74. Yes it would be possible. Cut along lines 1 and 2 as shown in figure A.

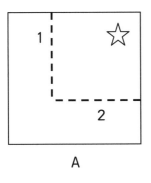

A

Remove that piece and rotate it to fit as shown in figure B.

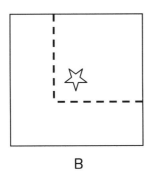

B

75.

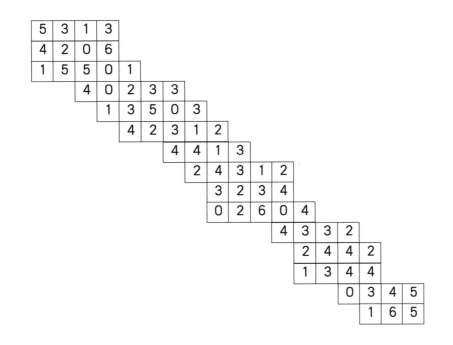

76. PREPOSITIONS

```
G  L  L  T  Q  Y  T  D  N  O  Y  E  B
N  T  D  D  G  R  M  G  T  T  G  Q  H
T  O  R  T  A  M  O  N  G  N  N  K  L
H  W  A  M  P  O  P  P  O  S  I  T  E
R  A  O  O  Z  E  N  Q  K  M  W  H  N
O  R  B  L  U  G  C  B  R  B  O  N  H
U  D  A  E  M  T  E  X  L  E  L  V  M
G  M  K  O  N  T  S  B  E  S  L  D  K
H  Q  R  T  W  E  B  I  K  I  O  J  E
G  F  N  E  A  R  A  L  D  D  F  V  F
N  W  E  W  F  C  H  T  W  E  O  L  R
X  N  R  N  M  K  G  R  H  B  X  J  M
G  Q  W  W  L  B  B  R  A  M  D  Q  L
```

77.

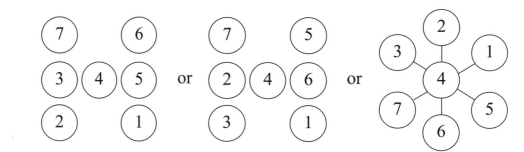

7   6   7   5   2
                            3   1
3 4 5 or 2 4 6 or   4
                            7   5
2   1   3   1   6

78. Fire
FIREPLACE
FIREWOOD
FIREFLY
FIREPROOF

79. △ = 2, ■ = 3, ○ = 5, ☆ = 6

80. Since the prince always tells the truth, he could not have made statement 1 or 2. That means the prince is No. 3. Since he states the jester is next to him, the jester is No. 2, leaving the princess (who lied this time) to be No. 1.

81. Park, West, Zoom, Rave, Gulp, Spit, Jeer, Bear

82. Here's one answer. Did you find another way to do this?

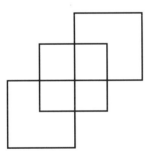

83. Remember, there may be more than one answer:

CHIP	CHUNK	CLASS
CLIP	CLUNK	GLASS
SLIP	CLINK	GRASS
SLAP	SLINK	GROSS
SLAM	SLICK	GROWS
	SLICE	GROWN

84.

12	16	10	2
5	3	14	8
7	9	1	6
4	13	15	11

85. H

The pairs are A-E (one hind leg has no stripes); B-I (the tops of the tails are missing); C-D (one front leg has fewer stripes); and F-G (the second stripe below the ear is shorter than the rest).

86. 6

Add the two wing numbers in each figure together. Then divide that sum by the tail number to arrive at the number in the circle.

87. Each row and column totals 18.

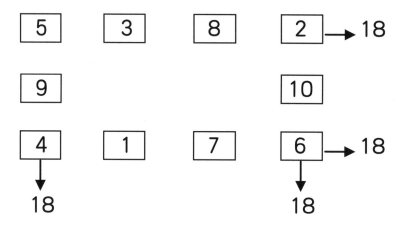

88. The answer is 22.

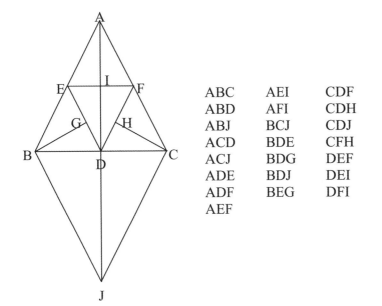

ABC   AEI   CDF
ABD   AFI   CDH
ABJ   BCJ   CDJ
ACD   BDE   CFH
ACJ   BDG   DEF
ADE   BDJ   DEI
ADF   BEG   DFI
AEF

89. Vision, Border, Garden, Pretty

90.

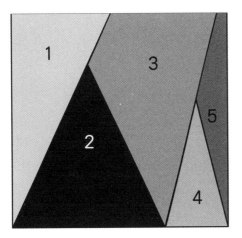

91.

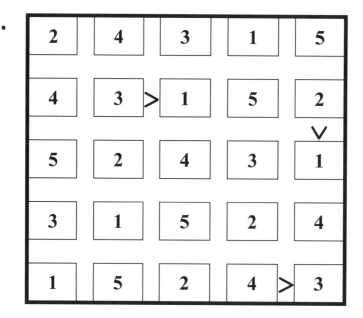

2	4	3	1	5
4	3 > 1		5	2
5	2	4	3	1
3	1	5	2	4
1	5	2	4 > 3	

92. The minimum number is six. Here's one way to do this but there are other ways.

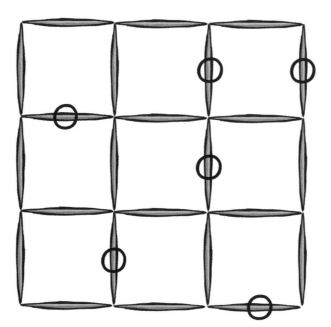

93. 12
Multiply the top two numbers in each triangle. Then divide that sum by the bottom number to get the number in the middle.

94. Marley will exit at block 1.

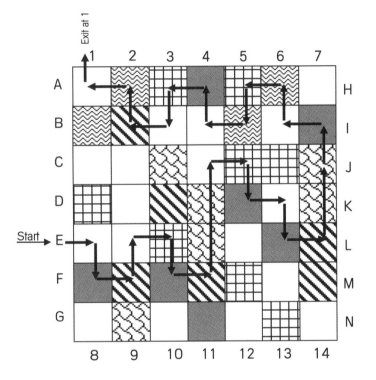

95. A will descend and B will rise.

96. Daddy Longlegs

97.

At The Zoo

98.

9	21	13	5	17
3	20	7	24	11
22	14	1	18	10
16	8	25	12	4
15	2	19	6	23

99. Remember, there may be more than one answer:

SORT	BLINK	HANDS
PORT	BRINK	BANDS
PART	BRICK	BENDS
PAST	TRICK	BEADS
PASS	TRACK	BEARS
	TRACE	BEARD

100. Acceptable is the odd one out. It is the only word that starts with a vowel, ends with a vowel, and has ten letters. The other words start and end with consonants, and have nine letters.